IN DEFENSE OF THE
US WORKING CLASS

ALSO BY MARY-ALICE WATERS

Author, editor, contributor

Our History Is Still Being Written: The Story of
Three Chinese Cuban Generals in the Cuban Revolution *(2017)*

Is Socialist Revolution in the US Possible? *(2016)*

"It's the Poor Who Face the Savagery of the US 'Justice' System"
(2016)

Los cosméticos, las modas y la explotación de la mujer *(2014)*

Cuba and Angola: Fighting for Africa's Freedom and Our Own
(2013)

Women in Cuba: The Making of a Revolution
within the Revolution *(2012)*

Capitalism and the Transformation of Africa *(2009)*

The Changing Face of US Politics *(2002)*

Pathfinder Was Born with the October Revolution *(2002)*

Cuba and the Coming American Revolution *(2001)*

Women's Liberation and the Line of March
of the Working Class *(1992)*

Che's Proletarian Legacy and Cuba's Rectification Process *(1991)*

1945: When US Troops Said 'No' *(1991)*

Thomas Sankara Speaks *(1988)*

Feminism and the Marxist Movement *(1972)*

Rosa Luxemburg Speaks *(1970)*

MARY-ALICE WATERS

In defense of the US working class

Pathfinder

NEW YORK   LONDON   MONTREAL   SYDNEY

Edited by Mary-Alice Waters

ISBN 978-1-60488-107-3
Library of Congress Control Number 2018965050
Manufactured in Canada

COVER DESIGN: Toni Gorton

FRONT COVER: Frankfort, Kentucky, April 2018. Teachers rally at state capitol against proposed cuts to pensions. (Alex Slitz/Associated Press)

BACK COVER: March in Jacksonville, Florida, October 2018, demands voting rights be restored to former prisoners. (Ithiell Yisrael/Florida Rights Restoration Coalition)

Pathfinder

www.pathfinderpress.com
E-mail: pathfinder@pathfinderpress.com

TABLE OF CONTENTS

ABOUT THE AUTHOR

Mary-Alice Waters, a member of the Socialist Workers Party National Committee since 1967, is president of Pathfinder Press and editor of *New International* magazine. She was won to revolutionary working-class politics in the early 1960s under the impact of the rising mass struggle that brought down the Jim Crow  structure of race segregation in the US, as well as by the advancing socialist revolution in Cuba. Waters joined the Young Socialist Alliance in 1962 and Socialist Workers Party in 1964. She has helped lead the SWP's work nationally and internationally, especially in defense of the Cuban Revolution as well as the fight for women's liberation.

Waters was YSA national secretary and then chairperson (1967–68). She covered the 1968 student-labor uprising in France for the *Militant* and edited that working-class newsweekly from 1969 through the early 1970s.

She has edited a series of more than thirty books on the Cuban Revolution, as well as more than a dozen other titles. Waters has spoken widely in the United States and around the world on the Cuban Revolution and its lessons for working people and youth everywhere.

PREFACE

Did the 2016 election of Donald Trump as US president indicate an increase in racism, xenophobia, anti-woman prejudice, and every other form of reaction among working people in the United States? Is that why millions of workers, of all races, voted for him?

Are working people in the United States capable of making a socialist revolution? Can we awaken to our own strength as we come together fighting for the interests of our class and our oppressed and exploited allies? Can we take state power out of the hands of the capitalist class, establish a workers and farmers government, and lead the reorganization of society in the interests of the vast majority?

These questions, which have been asked by many, not only in Cuba but in the US and around the world, are answered in the talk by Mary-Alice Waters published here. Waters, a member of the Socialist Workers Party's National Committee and president of Pathfinder Press, spoke at a conference in Havana, Cuba, that was part of the 2018 events celebrating May Day, the international day of the working class. Those activities culminated on May 1, when more than a million Cuban workers, farmers, students, and others poured into the streets of Havana and across the island in a show of support for their socialist revolution.

The talk was the first part of a special program on the

class struggle in the United States. It was followed by a panel titled, "From Clinton to Trump: How working people in the US are responding to the antilabor offensive of the bosses, their parties, and their government." The panelists were leaders and supporters of the Socialist Workers Party with years of experience in major industries and trade unions as well as on the land. They described the many intertwined forms of capitalist exploitation and oppression faced by working people in capitalist America.

Waters and members of the panel talked about the employers' speedup on the job, gutting of safety protections, and slashing of wages and pensions. The rising burden of health care costs. The cutbacks in funding for education, transportation, and other social necessities.

They described the devastating toll on the families of workers and farmers of seventeen years of war waged by Washington in Afghanistan, Iraq, Syria. The opioid addiction crisis and rising suicide rate among young adults in the prime of life. The despoiling of the environment. The staggering rates of incarceration, especially among workers who are African American, Latino, and Native American.

They reported the shrinking availability of abortion services for women. The growing number of farm bankruptcies. The student debt crisis facing millions of young people entering the workforce. The deportations of foreign-born workers. The attacks on constitutionally guaranteed rights of working people, including the right to vote.

Far more important, however, the speakers also explained how workers have fought back against this forty-year offensive by the employers and their government. They pointed especially to the teachers strike in West Virginia and the impetus it gave to a wave of strikes and protests by school personnel in the spring of 2018 that swept Oklahoma, Kentucky, Arizona, and other states.

The program on the US class struggle was a central feature of the Twelfth International May Day Scientific Conference, held April 24–26, 2018. The main sponsors were the Cuban History Institute and the Central Organization of Cuban Workers (CTC), the country's trade union federation. Most of the hundred thirty participants were from cities across Cuba. Others came from Mexico, Argentina, Chile, Colombia, the United States, Spain, and the United Kingdom. The event was held at a historic trade union and cultural center in Central Havana, the Cigar Workers Palace.

CTC general secretary Ulises Guilarte opened the conference with an address on challenges facing Cuban working people and their unions today. Those challenges take unique forms in Cuba, he explained, because "here the working class is in power." Leaders of Cuba's Commercial and Food Workers Union and the Tourism Workers Union, among others, gave additional reports. The three-day conference included more than twenty panel discussions on topics from the history of the workers movement in Cuba to the situation facing workers and farmers in Latin American countries today.

The program on the class struggle in the United States was held on the final day. Waters explained that what is driving working people—whether they voted in 2016 for Hillary Clinton, Donald Trump, or refused to vote for either one—is not an increase in reactionary attitudes and actions.

The opposite is true, she said. Among the US working classes "there is today greater openness than at any time in our political lives to thinking about and discussing what a socialist revolution could mean and why it just might be necessary. To consider the idea that our class is capable of shouldering the responsibility of state power and why we should do so."

You'd never know that from reading or watching the bourgeois media, Waters said, but we know it is true from our own experiences. It's what we have learned "firsthand from the men and women we meet as we go door to door in working-class neighborhoods of every racial and ethnic composition—cities, towns, and country—from one end of the US to the other, talking about these questions." We know it from discussions on the job with our co-workers, on picket lines, and at protest actions over issues from voting rights to police violence to the environment.

Is a socialist revolution in the US possible? Not only possible, Waters answered, but "even more important, revolutionary struggles by the toilers are inevitable." What is not inevitable, she said, is victory. That depends on the political clarity and, above all, "the caliber and experience of proletarian leadership."

Describing the revolutionary capacities of working people in the US, Waters drew on class-struggle experiences that are part of living memory. She pointed to the great labor organizing drives of the 1930s, as well as the mass Black-led struggle of the 1950s and '60s that brought down Jim Crow—the violent, institutionalized system of race segregation in the US South. Waters recalled the massive movement against Washington's war in Vietnam, which reached deep into the working class, including the millions in military uniform, shaking the confidence of the US rulers.

The panel that followed Waters's remarks included Jacob Perasso, a freight rail conductor and unionist from Albany, New York; Alyson Kennedy, a cashier at a Walmart store in Dallas, Texas, and for fourteen years an underground coal miner; Willie Head, a lifelong working farmer in south Georgia; Róger Calero from New York, who was part of strikes by meatpackers in Minnesota and coal miners in Utah; and Omari Musa from Washington, D.C., a veteran of union struggles in oil and rail and of the fight for Black rights.

Harry D'Agostino, a young worker and musician, was at the last minute unable to join the panel, but his written remarks were distributed to the audience.

Questions and discussion followed the program and continued informally for the rest of the afternoon. A number of participants said they especially appreciated the concrete information about job conditions and labor struggles in the US. They were amazed by the facts presented.

One of the participants from Mexico commented that what she had learned "completely changed my view of what is happening in the United States today."

~

The talk by Waters appears here along with brief biographies of the panelists and summaries of their remarks. Also reprinted is the transcript of a 1981 Radio Havana Cuba program explaining the fighting history of coal miners and the United Mine Workers of America (UMWA). Several of the speakers referred to that militant record and its living legacy in West Virginia and throughout the mountainous coal region of the eastern US. Copies of the broadcast, reprinted from coverage in the *Militant* newspaper at the time, were distributed to everyone at the conference.

~

The wave of teachers strikes ebbed with the end of the school year. As has happened so many times in US history, the momentum was broken and led into the dead-end of capitalist electoral politics as the November 2018 state and federal congressional elections approached. But struggles by working people continue.

Truckers organized by the Teamsters union at ports in Los Angeles and San Diego, California, have carried out actions demanding to be recognized as employees, not "independent contractors" with no guaranteed hours, wages, or unemployment benefits. As part of that fight, for the first time ever, the Teamsters leadership supported actions against the threat of deportation facing many of their members due to the US government's decision to end the Temporary Protected Status of more than 300,000 workers originally from Honduras, El Salvador, and Nicaragua as well as Haiti, Nepal and Sudan.

Working people across Florida mobilized to win restoration of voting rights for more than a million former prisoners there. The 64 percent margin in favor of that November ballot initiative—cast by voters of all skin colors and national origins—further belies liberals' notion of a rise of racist and rightist views among working people. Workers in Kentucky, Iowa, and other states where laws still restrict ex-prisoners' right to vote are organizing to build on this victory.

Thousands of UMWA-organized coal miners and other unionists rallied July 12, 2018, at the statehouse in Columbus, Ohio, to protest the owners' gutting of their pensions. Workers at McDonald's and other fast-food chains, many of them in their teens and early twenties, walked off the job in Detroit and other major cities October 4 to demand a base pay of $15 an hour. Sizable actions against killings of African American youth by cops have taken place in cities and towns across the country, from Pittsburgh to Dallas to Hoover, Alabama.

And as this book was being readied for the printers, some eight thousand union workers at four dozen Marriott hotels, from San Francisco and Honolulu to Chicago and Boston, walked off the job demanding higher pay and no hike in the steep medical insurance costs already passed on to them by the hotel owners. Their determined stance and rallying cry— "One job should be enough!"—has struck a chord among millions of US working people who also find themselves forced to work two or three jobs to survive.

For these and other working people gaining confidence in their own capacities to fight and win, this book helps point the road forward.

Martín Koppel
December 2018

ANOS DE PRINCIPIOS, UNIDAD E

Hundreds of thousands of workers, farmers, and youth marched in Havana May 1, 2018, expressing support for their socialist revolution.

The April 24–26, 2018, conference in Havana hosted by the Cuban History Institute and the Central Organization of Cuban Workers was part of the program of events celebrating May Day, the international day of the working class. More than a million Cubans poured into the streets across the island that day.

In defense of the US working class

MARY-ALICE WATERS

Thank you, René, for your generous introduction.

On behalf of all of us presenting this morning's program on the class struggle in the United States, I want to thank the Cuban History Institute, the Central Organization of Cuban Workers, and our hosts here at the Cigar Workers Palace for the privilege—and responsibility—you've given us.

Six months ago, when the president of the Cuban History Institute first asked us to prepare this session of the Twelfth International May Day Scientific Conference, I was skeptical. "We're neither professional historians nor academic researchers," I told him. "We're workers, trade unionists, farmers, communists, members and supporters of the Socialist Workers Party and Young Socialists. Will

Remarks to conference in Havana, Cuba, April 26, 2018, organized by the Cuban History Institute and the Central Organization of Cuban Workers (CTC). Waters was introduced by René González Barrios, president of the history institute.

Above: Members of panel on US class struggle. Program was part of International May Day conference in Havana, Cuba, April 2018. From left, Willie Head, Omari Musa, Alyson Kennedy, Jacob Perasso, Mary-Alice Waters. At podium (not seen) is Róger Calero.

Above: Part of audience. Most of the 130 participants were from cities across Cuba; several came from elsewhere in Latin America, the US, and Europe.

Below left: René González Barrios, president of Cuban History Institute, addresses conference. **Right:** Ulises Guilarte, general secretary of Central Organization of Cuban Workers, gives opening report.

our participation be appropriate?"

Each of you has a copy of the brief biographies we prepared on the members of our panel.[1] I won't repeat what's in those notes, except to say that those you will hear from today have lived and worked in every part of the United States—on the land and in jobs from coal mines, oil refineries and railroads, to garment shops, construction sites, slaughterhouses, auto assembly lines, warehouses, and retail giants like Walmart—the largest private employer in the US today with 1.5 million workers on the payroll (and another eight hundred thousand worldwide).

As class-conscious workers, of course, we are part of every social, political, and cultural battle at the center of the class struggle in the US. And that starts with opposition to every act of aggression, every war waged openly or covertly by US imperialism.

René listened patiently to all our hesitations. Then he just smiled and said: "That's what we need. At the history institute we talk to many who study the working class. We also want to hear from those who *are* workers."

So here we are, and we look forward to your questions, your doubts and comments, and above all a fruitful discussion.

I can assure you in advance that what we have to say will not be what you regularly hear, see, or read in either the "mass media," or through what is now known as "social media." I prefer "bourgeois media" as the more accurate label for *both*.

I will focus my remarks on two questions we are often asked.

First. Did the 2016 electoral victory of Donald Trump

---

1. See pp. 47–56.

register a rise in racism, xenophobia, misogyny, and every other form of ideological reaction among working people in the US? Is that why tens of millions of workers of all races voted for him?

Second. Is a socialist revolution in the US really possible? Or are those like ourselves, who answer with an unhesitating "Yes," a new variety of utopian socialist fools, however well meaning?

A giant begins to stir

The clearest and most demonstrative answer to the first question is being given right now from West Virginia to Oklahoma, from Kentucky to Arizona and beyond by tens of thousands of teachers and other public workers in states Trump carried by a large margin in 2016.

Less than two months ago, in February and March, in the state of West Virginia, one of the most significant strikes in a quarter century exploded onto the national scene. Some thirty-five thousand teachers, janitors, bus drivers, cafeteria workers, and other public school employees walked off the job together, defying past court rulings denying public employees the right to strike. With overwhelming support from their communities, they closed down the schools in all fifty-five counties in the state. *Every single one!* That surprised even the fighting teachers.

The action came after years of ruling-class budget cuts that slashed funding for students' meals, textbooks, school supplies, building maintenance, salaries of teachers and other employees, and eliminated many so-called extra-curricular activities such as sports, art, music, and other programs children need to learn and grow.

West Virginia is the historic heart of coal country in the United States, the site of some of the hardest fought labor battles in US history, such as those described by Radio

Havana in the program you all have a transcript of.[2] West Virginia has also long been one of the most economically ravaged areas of the country. It is even more so today.

> **Over the last four decades, the coal bosses and their government have waged a concerted assault on the lives and living standards of working people.**

Over the last four decades, the coal bosses and their government, determined to drive down the owners' labor costs and break the back of the United Mine Workers union (UMWA), have waged a concerted assault on the lives and living standards of working people.

Coal companies have closed hundreds of mines throughout the mountainous Appalachian region as they've shifted capital to oil, natural gas, and other fossil-fuel energy sources. The bulk of coal production today comes from surface coal mines in western regions of the United States—mines where the owners have successfully kept the work force unorganized. Their only concern is to increase their rate of profit as they employ fewer miners.

Some fifty years ago the UMWA, long the most powerful union in the country, represented 70 percent of coal miners. That figure today stands at 21 percent.

We don't have time to tell the story of how the health clinics throughout the coal fields, won by the miners in prior struggles, have been closed as the coal bosses dumped their contract obligations to fund them. Or why black-lung disease, the deadly scourge of miners, driven back in the 1970s and 1980s, is once again rapidly expanding throughout the

2. See pp. 57–64.

region. It is now hitting younger miners in an even more virulent form thanks to lack of protection from the smaller, more dangerous coal and silica dust produced by new mining technology.

Nor can we describe how the mining companies have used bankruptcy proceedings, court rulings, and corporate "restructurings" to declare union contracts invalid, dump pension obligations, and eliminate UMWA-controlled mine safety committees that were fought for and conquered in previous battles. Through those union committees, miners themselves asserted their power to shut down work on *any* shift in face of *any* unsafe condition.

You will hear more about these questions later in the program from one of our panelists, Alyson Kennedy, who worked fourteen years as an underground coal miner.

The consequences of this decades-long assault are registered in the statistics.

West Virginia today has the lowest median household income of all fifty states in the union save one, Mississippi. In only three states—Oklahoma, South Dakota, and Mississippi—do teachers earn less than in West Virginia.

Measured by official US government figures that include so-called discouraged workers—those who haven't been able to find a job for so long that they've temporarily given up—unemployment in West Virginia is third highest in the country; it topped 10 percent in 2017.

The state is a center of the drug addiction crisis in the US. It has the highest opioid overdose rate in the country. And the drug crisis is still accelerating, registered most forcefully in one fact: life expectancy in the United States has actually *dropped* for three consecutive years in 2015–17.

To this picture you have to add the not-so-hidden toll of Washington's endless wars, the burden of which, as always, falls most heavily on working-class and farm families in the most depressed regions of the country. Among veterans of the wars in Afghanistan, Iraq, Syria, and elsewhere, the suicide rate is twenty a day. Yes, you heard that right. *Twenty a day.*

We could add more to this picture, but it's not necessary.

The point is that without understanding the devastation of the lives of working-class families in regions like West Virginia (and there are many others from New Mexico and Ohio and Kentucky to New Hampshire), without understanding the vast increase since the 2008 financial crisis in *class* inequality (including the accelerating inequality *within* the working classes and middle layers) *you won't be able to understand what's happening in the United States.*

You have to compare this panorama of carnage with the lives of the upper layers of the middle class to be found in places like Silicon Valley, and the more exclusive (far from the *most* exclusive) neighborhoods of population centers like New York, Washington, and San Francisco.

This devastation facing working people is not only the consequence of the worldwide capitalist crisis of production and trade, which began in the mid-1970s and is still deepening. It is the consequence of the *policies* initiated by the Democratic Party administration of the two Clintons in the 1990s and pursued with equal vigor by the Republican administration of George W. Bush and the Democratic administration of Barack Obama.

• The elimination of federal aid to children of single mothers and drastic cuts in other social welfare programs on all levels.

• Policies and legislation disguised with names like a "war on drugs" and calls for more "criminal justice" that have made the United States the country with the highest incarceration rate in the world. With a little over 4 percent of the world's population the US has some 25 percent of all prisoners on earth. It was among those prisoners, we should add, that our five Cuban brothers lived and carried out their political work for some sixteen years.[3]

All these questions are explained and documented in several of the most widely read books published by Pathfinder Press that are available on the table that many of you have already visited: *The Clintons' Anti-Working-Class Record* and *Are They Rich Because They're Smart?*—both by Jack Barnes, the national secretary of the Socialist Workers Party, and *"It's the Poor Who Face the Savagery of the US 'Justice' System"* in which the Cuban Five, as they are known around the world, talk about their experiences as part of the working class behind bars in the United States.

West Virginia workers fight back
Often when we explain these social realities to working people here in Cuba (and elsewhere), they ask, "Why does

---

3. In September 1998 the Clinton administration announced that a "Cuban spy network" had been uncovered in Florida and the FBI had arrested ten of its members. In June 2001, the five defendants put on trial—Fernando González, René González, Antonio Guerrero, Gerardo Hernández, and Ramón Labañino—were each convicted of "conspiracy to act as an unregistered foreign agent." Guerrero, Hernández, and Labañino were also convicted of "conspiracy to commit espionage," and Hernández of "conspiracy to commit murder." Sentences ranged from fifteen years to a double life term plus fifteen years for Hernández.

The five revolutionaries—today "Heroes of the Republic of Cuba"—had accepted assignments to keep the Cuban government informed about counterrevolutionary groups in the US planning terrorist attacks against Cuba. The dignity and strength of the Five themselves, the untiring efforts by the Cuban government, and a broad international campaign demanding their release finally won the freedom of the last three—Hernández, Labañino and Guerrero—on December 17, 2014. On the same day, Presidents Raúl Castro and Barack Obama announced the restoration of diplomatic relations between the two countries, severed by Washington some fifty-five years earlier.

anyone accept this? Why hasn't there been any resistance?"

Our answer is always the same: "There *is* resistance. Workers never stop looking for ways to fight back—and *act* when they find ways." But if you are not part of the working class, you're not aware of what is happening until it explodes.

"In the best traditions of trade unionism—and a precursor of the fighting labor movement that will again be built—the strike took on elements of a genuine social movement."

No worker goes on strike until they've exhausted other remedies. Until they feel they have no other choice.

The West Virginia teachers strike was just that kind of volcanic eruption. It seemed to come out of nowhere, but it had been building for years. Its roots were deep.

When the teachers and other school employees walked out, when they saw the strength of their numbers, their confidence and determination soared too. With support from their pupils, families, unions, and churches—and a living memory of the many bitter strikes fought by the miners—they organized emergency food services for the students and strikers. Daytime activities for the children were put in place. Clothing and funds were collected, and more.

In the best traditions of trade unionism—and a precursor of the fighting labor movement that will again be built—the strike took on elements of a genuine social movement, battling for the needs of the entire working class and its allies.

"What we're seeing is a class of people rising up," one

"In West Virginia one of the most significant labor battles in a quarter century exploded onto the national scene."

CHRIS DORST/ASSOCIATED PRESS

EMMA JOHNSON/MILITANT

LILY ALTAVENA/AZCENTRAL

Teachers, bus drivers, cafeteria workers, and custodians closed schools in all 55 counties, winning pay raise for all state employees. Strike took on elements of a social movement fighting for needs of working people.

Above: Strikers rally at state capitol in Charleston, West Virginia, February 2018.

Left: Volunteers at church in Hurricane, West Virginia, pack lunches for students who rely on meals they get at school. Similar efforts were organized across the state.

Right: Phoenix, Arizona, March 2018. Rally by striking teachers. Handmade signs at actions everywhere testified to impact of West Virginia strike.

Teachers strikes, Waters said, were "living refutation of the portrait of working-class 'backwardness' painted by middle-class liberals and the radical left. It's not only Donald Trump they hope to impeach. Their target—and what they have begun to fear—is that class of people who are rising up, many of whom voted for Trump."

Top: School bus drivers and supporters picket depot during nine-day strike, Hurricane, West Virginia, March 2018. Sign at right protests cuts in medical coverage announced by state's Public Employee Insurance Agency.

CHIP BOK/CREATORS.COM

striking worker proudly told a reporter.

And he was right. These were the men and women whom Hillary Clinton during her presidential campaign so contemptuously labeled "a basket of deplorables." People from the "backward" (that was her word!) expanses of the country between New York and California. People she described as "racist, sexist, homophobic, xenophobic," and especially women, "married white women" who, she told audiences, were too weak to stand up to "pressure to vote the way your husband, your boss, your son" tells you to.

Is it any wonder Trump won West Virginia by a vote of 69 percent to 27 percent for Clinton?

The *better* class of people who engaged in this struggle across West Virginia not only kept every school closed for nine days. They sent thousands of demonstrators to occupy the state capitol day after day. Midway through the walkout, teachers rejected their union officialdom's call to accept the governor's promise of a deal. *They'd heard promises before.* They stayed out until they forced the legislature to pass, and the governor to sign into law, a 5 percent pay raise—not only for school personnel, but for every single state employee.

A confident mass of red-shirted victors marched out of the state capitol building shouting, "Who made history? We made history!"

And as word spread across the country, teachers in Oklahoma, Kentucky, Arizona, and other states were preparing their own strike actions. "Don't make us go West Virginia on you!" became their battle cry.

Of all that, you'll hear more from the panel later this morning.

What has happened in West Virginia is a living refutation of the portrait of working-class bigotry and "backwardness" painted, almost without exception, by a broad spectrum of middle-class liberals and much of the radical left in the US, and around the world as well. It is not only Donald Trump they obsessively hope to impeach. Their target—and the object they have begun to fear—is that class of people who are rising up, many of whom voted for Trump.

What's behind the actions of tens of thousands of working people like these is not hatred of Mexicans, Muslims, African Americans, or a desire to keep women at home, barefoot and pregnant. Just look at the photos on display here of the women in West Virginia, Kentucky, Arizona and elsewhere who have been in the front ranks of the teachers' struggles!

Workers engaged in these fights are not clamoring for a border wall, groping women, or marching with KKK hoods and burning crosses. They are demanding dignity and respect for themselves and their families, and for all working people like them.

And they have nothing but distrust and growing hatred for those they call "the political class," both Republican and Democrat, in Washington and in every state capital in the country. That's why chants of "Drain the swamp!" resonated far beyond those who voted for Trump. It's not reactionary attitudes that are driving most working people. But it's not independent class political consciousness either. That can only develop over time through *large-scale working-class actions on picket lines and in the streets.*

We don't pretend to know the pace at which such struggles will develop or the forms they will take, but we do know they will be marked by the kind of class solidarity that flowered in West Virginia.

If you remember even one thing from our program here today, I hope it will be this:

Among working people in the United States today there

is greater openness than at any time in our political lives to thinking about and discussing what a socialist revolution could mean and why it just might be necessary. To consider the idea that our class is capable of shouldering the responsibility of state power and why we should do so. To realize that we can ourselves become different human beings in the process.

That political openness, that political interest, is as great among those who voted for Trump as among those who voted for Clinton, or among the record number who couldn't bring themselves to vote for either presidential candidate.

> **Revolutionary struggles by the toilers are inevitable. They will be forced upon us by the crisis-driven assaults of the propertied classes.**

We don't know this from polls or news reports in the bourgeois media. We know it from our own experiences, and from our kin scattered across the United States. We know it firsthand from the men and women we meet as we go door to door in working-class neighborhoods of every racial and ethnic composition—cities, towns, and country—from one end of the United States to the other, talking about these questions with thousands of working people. With whoever comes to the door.

A socialist revolution in the US?

That brings us to the second question. Is a socialist revolution in the US really possible?

Two months ago, we were asked that question by a student here in Havana at the foreign ministry's Higher Institute for Foreign Relations (ISRI). He didn't believe it, he said. The economic and military strength of Washington is far too great—and the working class far too backward. US imperialism, he insisted, will have to be defeated "from the outside."

We in the Socialist Workers Party are certainly among a small minority, even among those who call themselves socialists, who say without hesitation, "Yes, socialist revolution is possible in the United States."

And I would add, no liberating movement can ever be imposed "from the outside" *on any country*. It can only be victorious through the actions of millions.

We say not only is socialist revolution in the US possible. Even more important, revolutionary struggles by the toilers are *inevitable*. They will be forced upon us by the crisis-driven assaults of the propertied classes—as we've just seen in West Virginia. And they will be intertwined, as always, with the example of the resistance and struggles of other oppressed and exploited producers around the globe.

What is *not* inevitable is the outcome. That is where political clarity, organization, prior experience, discipline, and, above all, the caliber and experience of proletarian leadership are decisive.

Our confidence comes from the class struggles we ourselves have been part of, as well as what we learned firsthand from the battle-tested workers who recruited us to the communist movement. I will give you just three examples.

Great labor conquests of the '30s
Those who recruited my generation were among the founders of the first Communist Party in the United States in 1919. They were delegates to the founding congresses of

the Communist International. They were leaders of the great labor battles of the 1930s, struggles that in a few short years swept past the craft-divided business unions of the American Federation of Labor to build a powerful social movement that organized industrial unions in virtually every basic industry.

> **More than any other labor experience, it is the Teamsters organizing drive of the 1930s that taught us what the US working class is capable of as it awakens in struggle.**

By the high point in the late 1940s some 35 percent of the privately employed working class was unionized, up from 7 percent in 1930 (a number close to the 6.5 percent of private-sector employees who are union members today). The lessons we learned from the speed and power of that transformation—including the pitched battles not only with employers' goons and police, but fascist gangs and National Guard troops sent in to break strikes—all that is part of our basic education.

The rise of the CIO, the Congress of Industrial Organizations, is told in rich detail in one of the books you'll find on the Pathfinder table at the back, *Labor's Giant Step* by Art Preis. He was one of the *Militant's* principal labor reporters for many years.

What I want to call special attention to here today, however, is the most far-reaching and politically significant of the labor struggles of the 1930s—the over-the-road union-organizing drive of the Teamsters, the truck drivers union. It was an organizing campaign that began in the North Central city of Minneapolis in 1934 and, by its high point in 1938–39, had been spread across an area nearly the size of the Indian subcontinent. Yes, the Indian subcontinent! The rich history and lessons of this campaign are recorded in four remarkable books—*Teamster Rebellion, Teamster Power, Teamster Politics,* and *Teamster Bureaucracy.* And we're pleased that today, here at this conference, we have all four volumes in print in Spanish for the first time ever.

Farrell Dobbs, the author of the Teamster series, was in his twenties, shoveling coal in a Minneapolis depot, when he emerged as a leader of the 1934 strikes that turned that city into a union town. He was the central organizer of the campaign that brought a quarter million over-the-road truckers into the union—from Tennessee to North Dakota, from Texas to Ohio. He resigned as general organizer of the Teamsters union national staff in 1940 to become labor secretary of the Socialist Workers Party, and he was sent to prison during World War II along with seventeen other leaders of General Drivers Local 544-CIO and the Socialist Workers Party for organizing labor opposition to the imperialist war aims of the US government. He later served as national secretary of the SWP for twenty years.

More than any other labor experience, it is the Teamsters organizing drive that taught us what the US working class is capable of as it awakens in struggle. It taught us how quickly the working class can learn the meaning of class political independence, proletarian internationalism, and begin to transform the union movement into an instrument of revolutionary struggle for the entire class and its allies.

The experiences we learned from involved organizing a *general* drivers union, an industrial union uniting workers from coal and food delivery truckers to taxi drivers, warehouse workers, and over-the-road drivers. They in-

"The principal lesson for labor militants to derive from the Minneapolis experience is not that, under an adverse relationship of forces, the workers can be overcome, but that, with proper leadership, they can overcome." —*Farrell Dobbs*

Strikes won by Teamsters in Minneapolis, Minnesota, in 1934, along with hard-fought victories in battles by California dockworkers and Ohio auto parts workers, set the example that led to the organization of auto, steel, and virtually all basic industry before the end of the decade.

Above: Striking Teamsters defend themselves from bloody assaults by police and "special deputies." In May 1934 hundreds of workers in the Minneapolis market district routed the cops as well as the bosses' thugs.

volved organizing the unemployed, farmers, women, and owner-operator independent truckers as allies. They included launching and training a disciplined Union Defense Guard that stopped in its tracks a fascist recruitment effort promoted by the bosses.

These experiences included the broadening international horizons of union militants as they followed events in Germany, China, and Spain and took on gangs of Jew-hating thugs. There was growing awareness of the need for workers to enter the political arena as an independent class force, with their own party.

That rapid advance came to an end in 1939–40 as the pressures of Washington's intensifying imperialist war drive came down on the labor movement. But as Dobbs writes in his "Afterword" to *Teamster Bureaucracy*, "The principal lesson for labor militants to derive from the Minneapolis experience is not that, under an adverse relationship of forces, the workers can be overcome, but that, with proper leadership, they can overcome."

And that is the principal lesson we also learned from the men and women who—under Fidel—led the Cuban Revolution to victory.

Bringing down Jim Crow

None of us on this panel today lived through the great labor battles of the '30s. But several of us *were* part of the generations transformed by our experiences as part of another profoundly revolutionary, working-class struggle—the mass movement of the 1950s and '60s that brought down the Jim Crow system of institutionalized race segregation in the US South. That successful fight forever changed social relations in the North as well as the South, including within the working class and unions.

That is the second example I'll draw on to explain our

confidence that socialist revolution in the US is possible.

The roots of the battle that brought down Jim Crow are to be found in the decades of resistance to the counter-revolutionary violence and terror against African Americans that reigned throughout the South following the abolition of slavery there in 1863 during the US Civil War. That was part of the Second American Revolution. The popular revolutionary governments—in some cases Black led—that took power in the states of the former slavocracy were soon betrayed by the rising forces of finance capital. By 1877 Radical Reconstruction, as it was known, had been drowned in blood.

Seventy-five years later, however, the objective conditions in the late 1950s that gave rise to another powerful wave of struggle were quite different. The revolutionary struggle that was popularly known as the Civil Rights movement was, above all, the product of:

• The mass workers struggles of the 1930s, which fought to racially integrate the workforce in auto, steel, trucking, and many other industries.

• The social convulsions of World War II, which included the exodus from the rural South and the accelerated incorporation of millions of African American workers, both male and female, into industry and other urban employment, North and South. That was part of what is known as the Great Migration that had begun during the first imperialist world war. It included the recruitment of hundreds of thousands of soldiers who were Black to serve in segregated, dangerous, so-called noncombat units of the US armed forces during World War II.

• The desegregation of the US armed forces that began in the years of "peace" between the atomic bombing of Japan in 1945 and the Washington-organized invasion, partition, and occupation of Korea in 1950. In 1951, faced by

The social convulsions of World War II were one of the roots of the mass proletarian movement that brought down Jim Crow segregation. Hundreds of thousands of African American workers and farmers served in segregated, dangerous 'noncombat' units of US military. Millions were drawn into industry and other urban employment, North and South.

Top: New York, 1942. Rally called to end segregation in the US armed forces, to discrimination in war industries, and to condemn frame-up and execution of Virginia sharecropper Odell Waller.

Bottom: Clovis, New Mexico, March 1943. Rail workers Almeta Williams, Beatrice Davis, Liza Goss, and Abbie Caldwell were among women hired for industrial jobs previously closed to them.

determined resistance from Korean and supporting Chinese troops, as well as growing disaffection among Black soldiers in segregated units, the army's combat units were also desegregated.

• The victorious wave of national liberation movements that swept the colonial world during and after World War II, from China, Korea, Vietnam, and Indonesia to India, Africa, and the Caribbean. This included the Cuban Revolution, which marked the furthest advance of those national liberation struggles.

• The naked hypocrisy and moral bankruptcy of the US rulers, who claimed to have instigated and pursued that second worldwide slaughter for "democracy," "freedom," and "equality."

For my generation, and several others of us here this morning, the years of mass struggle that overturned the American prototype of apartheid were a school of popular revolutionary action, *our* school.

That's when we learned discipline. When we learned the power we had, not as individuals, but in our numbers and, above all, our organization. When we learned how to engage within the movement in heated, yet civil debate. When we learned to be political, not naïve, as we joined the inevitable battles between conflicting class forces raging within the movement for Black rights.

One of the myths of the mass struggle to bring down Jim Crow is that it was a pacifist movement. That all those involved were opposed, in principle, to taking up arms in self-defense against the violence of the Ku Klux Klan, White Citizens Council, and other vigilante outfits deeply intertwined with the Democratic Party and police departments across the South and parts of the border states.

The record shows otherwise. It was workers with military training and combat experience in World War II and Korea who organized themselves as the Deacons for Defense and Justice in Louisiana, and a chapter of the NAACP in Monroe, North Carolina, to protect their communities and their children who were marching. Martin Luther King was protected by well-organized security.

> **The years of mass struggle that overturned the American prototype of apartheid were a school of popular revolutionary action, our school.**

Above all, we identified with and learned from Malcolm X, as he more and more consciously charted a revolutionary, an internationalist, and then, yes, a working-class course. As he charted a course to join forces with those the world over, whatever their skin color, who understood that we are fighters in a worldwide conflict "between those who want freedom, justice and equality for everyone and those who want to continue the systems of exploitation."

For many of us, it was that mass, Black, proletarian movement in the United States, combined at the same time with the example given us by the workers and farmers of Cuba and their advancing revolution, that instilled *our* generation with unshakable confidence in the revolutionary capacities of working people.

The story of how those two revolutionary struggles came together for us is told in one of the most important books you will find on the Pathfinder table at the back, *Cuba and the Coming American Revolution* by Jack Barnes.

"The greatest obstacle to the line of march of the toilers," Jack says in those pages, "is the tendency, promoted and perpetuated by the exploiting classes, for working people to underestimate ourselves, to underestimate what we can accomplish, to doubt our own worth."

What the workers and farmers of Cuba showed us is that with class solidarity, political consciousness, courage, focused and persistent efforts at education, and a revolutionary leadership of a caliber like that in Cuba—a leadership tested and forged in combat, in sacrifice, over years—it is possible to stand up to enormous might and numbers that initially seem to pose insurmountable odds—*and win.* And then to accelerate the building of a truly *new* society, led by the only class capable of doing so.

That was the foundation of the political education of my generation.

Vietnam and imperialist war

As the mass proletarian struggle against Jim Crow triumphed, our confidence in the revolutionary capacities of the US working class deepened with the third example I'll point to. That was the battle to put an end to the US rulers' war against the people of Vietnam. We never doubted that the Vietnamese people—and those of us determined to defend their fight for national sovereignty and unification—would win.

In the course of that struggle, as the mobilizations against the war grew to involve millions, the widening fissures in the fabric of US society struck fear in the hearts of the US rulers.

Massive revolts erupted in the Black ghettos of major cities in the North, culminating in those that spread to virtually every US city in 1968 following the assassination of Martin Luther King. It was a cold-blooded political assassination in the midst of a strike by sanitation workers in Memphis, Tennessee, for whom King was rallying support.

In an effort to intimidate and quell protest actions against the war as well as in the ghettos, the US rulers more and

"The mass Black proletarian movement fighting Jim Crow segregation in the US, combined with the example set by the workers and farmers of Cuba, instilled our generation with unshakable confidence in the revolutionary capacities of working people."

RADIO REBELDE

Above: Montgomery, Alabama, December 1955. First mass meeting supporting boycott of city transit system over laws that forced Blacks to sit at back of the bus. The Black rights movement grew to millions in the US and brought down apartheid-like system of race segregation throughout the South.

Below: Havana, February 1962. One million demonstrate their support for the Second Declaration of Havana, being read by Fidel Castro. With the revolutionary victory at the Bay of Pigs (Playa Girón) the year before—Washington's first military defeat in the Americas—the Cuban people had set an example for the world that "revolution is possible," Castro said.

more often resorted to mobilizing National Guard troops. In May 1970, as demonstrations of unprecedented size rocked the US in opposition to Washington's invasion of Cambodia, along Vietnam's border, two students at Jackson State University in Mississippi and four students at Kent State University in Ohio were shot dead by National Guard forces occupying their campuses. The demonstrations spread further and reached deeper.

The US rulers and their servants were profoundly shaken by the spread of mass opposition to the Vietnam War not just among students and growing millions of workers but increasingly within the ranks of the US draftee army, especially those being sent to fight in Vietnam. The tide turned.

This was what the bourgeois political crisis known as Watergate and ouster of President Richard Nixon was really all about—the tremors of fear among the US rulers.

It is life experiences such as these that have taught us something about the political dynamics that will inevitably be part of a victorious American socialist revolution.

$\sim$

One final point.

The world we are living in today is not headed toward a future of capitalist peace and prosperity. To think otherwise you'd have to believe that the ruling families of the imperialist world and their financial wizards have found a way to "manage" capitalism in crisis. That they've discovered the means to preclude shattering financial collapses and breakdowns of production, trade, and employment.

You'd have to believe that the credit crisis that exploded as recently as 2007–08 was an aberration and won't happen again, with even more devastating consequences for working people.

"US rulers were profoundly shaken by the mass opposition to the Vietnam War, including within the ranks of the draftee army."

San Francisco, October 1968. Five hundred active-duty soldiers, some risking court-martial for marching in uniform, lead demonstration of 15,000 against the war in Vietnam.

"As the struggle against Jim Crow triumphed," said Waters, "our confidence in the revolutionary capacities of the US working class deepened during the battle to put an end to the US rulers' war against the people of Vietnam. We never doubted that the Vietnamese people—and those of us determined to defend their fight—would win."

The opposite is the truth.

The crisis of finance capital is not a short-term cyclical adjustment. World capitalism's profit rates have been on a long downward curve since the mid-1970s—more than four decades. Do any of us believe, under the domination of breakdown-ridden financial and banking capital, that world capitalism is entering a sustained period of increased investment in the expansion of industrial capacity and massive hiring of workers?

> **"Through the coming battles class consciousness, confidence, and leadership capacity will develop among working people, unevenly but apace."**

All evidence points in the other direction.

We have entered what will be decades of economic, financial, and social convulsions, of intensifying rivalries among capitalist state powers. Decades of sharpening class conflicts and devastating bloody wars like those in Iraq, Afghanistan, Syria, and more.

The coming years *will* end in World War III—inevitably—*if* the only class capable of doing so, *the working class*, fails to take state power. If we fail to take the power to wage war out of the hands of the imperialist rulers, in the United States above all.

But for us, a sober and realistic assessment of what lies ahead is reason neither for panic nor demoralization and despair. To the contrary. The years that are coming will also bring increasingly organized resistance—worldwide—by growing vanguards of working people pushed to the wall by the capitalists' drive to intensify the exploitation of working people in order to reverse their declining rate of profit.

"Revolutionary struggles are inevitable. They will be forced upon us by the assaults of the propertied classes and intertwined with the resistance of other exploited producers around the globe."

Above: Southwest France, December 2018. "Urgent. Purchasing power, dignity for all," says sign at protest. For weeks working people from towns and rural areas across France put on yellow vests (required by law in every car) in actions demanding an end to fuel-tax increase, pension cuts, and miserly minimum wage. Government was forced to retreat.

Below: Saigon, now Ho Chi Minh City, April 30, 1975. Victorious national liberation combatants enter grounds of presidential palace as final US forces flee by helicopter.

It is through those struggles that class consciousness, as well as confidence and leadership capacity, will develop among working people—unevenly but apace.

And time is on *our* side—not theirs.

On March 13, 1961, barely a month before the victorious battle of Playa Girón, or the Bay of Pigs debacle as it is known in the US, Fidel Castro spoke to tens of thousands of Cuban workers, farmers, and youth preparing to meet the invasion we all knew was inevitable. Answering Washington's illusions that the attempted invasion would install in Cuba a government subservient to the US rulers, Fidel told the cheering crowd: "There will be a victorious revolution in the United States before a victorious counterrevolution in Cuba."

His words were not empty bravado. Fidel *never* stooped to demagogy. Nor was he gazing in a crystal ball, pretending to divine the future. We, and the revolutionary people of Cuba, understood him well. He was speaking as a leader offering—*advancing*—a line of struggle, a line of march, for our lifetimes. He was, as always, addressing Lenin's question, "What is to be done?"

In North America—and Cuba as well—each succeeding generation of revolutionaries has carried those words on our banner.

The political capacities and revolutionary potential of workers and farmers in the US are today as utterly discounted by the ruling families and their servants as were those of the Cuban toilers at Playa Girón.

And just as wrongly.

From Clinton to Trump:
How US working people have fought back

Biographies and remarks of panel participants

MAYKEL ESPINOSA/JUVENTUD REBELDE

Panel at April 2018 conference in Havana, Cuba. From left, Róger Calero (at podium), Víctor García (translator), Willie Head, Omari Musa, Alyson Kennedy, and Jacob Perasso.

"From Clinton to Trump: How US working people are responding to the antilabor offensive of the bosses, their parties and their government." That was the title of the second part of the program on the class struggle in the US at the April 24–26, 2018, conference in Havana.

Members of the panel included a working farmer and four other workers with years of experience in different industries. Each made brief remarks detailing the consequences for working people of the bosses' four-decades-long offensive to boost "productivity" and their profit rates. Even more importantly, the panel members described some of the political, social, and labor struggles in which they and their coworkers have fought.

Brief biographical notes introducing each panel member were given to everyone present. Those notes appear below, along with summaries of remarks each of them made.

Alyson Kennedy. Alyson is a 14-year veteran union coal miner. She was among the first wave of women who in the 1970s and '80s broke through the barriers that coal bosses used to exclude them from underground mining jobs. She has been part of United Mine Workers battles in coal fields from West Virginia and Alabama to Utah. Alyson was the Socialist Workers Party candidate for president in 2016 and lives in Dallas, Texas, where she works at the international retail chain Walmart.

At the Havana conference, Kennedy highlighted some of the fighting history of the United Mine Workers of America (UMWA) including the successful struggle waged by the rank-and-file Miners for Democracy movement in the 1970s to win control of the union. The new union leadership then established the right of the ranks to vote on contracts. The strengthened union fought for and won union safety committees with the right to shut down production under dangerous conditions, and other key demands.

During the same years new federal equal-employment-opportunity laws obliged the coal bosses to allow women to work as underground miners. Kennedy explained how women miners learned to stand up to sexist harassment and other measures promoted by the coal bosses to drive them out of the mines, and how the women won union backing and support from fellow miners who were men. She described how the incorporation of women into the workforce strengthened the UMWA.

Kennedy also described the twenty-five thousand–strong mobilization of striking teachers and other school personnel in Oklahoma she had been part of three weeks earlier. In a state with no tradition of labor action like West Virginia's, teachers shut down the schools for nine days, winning a pay raise and increased school funding.

The Oklahoma strike was the strongest of the wave of teachers' actions that drew added energy from the example set by the West Virginia working class. Kennedy explained that, like teachers, many of her coworkers, as well as many customers, at Walmart work more than one job to survive. They identified with and supported the teachers' fight.

Willie Head. Willie is a longtime family farmer from south Georgia, a veteran of the century and a half of battles by farmers who are Black to keep their land. For twelve years he served as vice-president of the People's Tribunal in Valdosta, Georgia, a community organization that fought to bring to justice a policeman who beat to death a prisoner in custody whose hands were tied behind his back. Like most small farmers in the US, throughout his life Willie has worked many nonfarm jobs, union and nonunion, to pay the bills and keep farming.

Head described the police violence and killings of African Americans in the rural South and the work of the Valdosta

People's Tribunal, which he called his "first frontline fight with the US court system."

A century ago African American farmers owned more than 16 million acres of land in the US, he noted. Today that figure stands at 2.5 million acres. Head detailed the long court battle, begun in 1992, by more than twenty-five thousand farmers who are Black against the discrimination they face from banks, courts, and the federal government's Department of Agriculture. All these forces bring pressure to bear on farmers who are Black to give up and sell their land. He described how a court ruling not only left farmers like himself who had "won" worse off than before, but also made them ineligible for any Department of Agriculture loans or assistance.

Head described the kinds of jobs he had worked to survive, including one that involved a daily drive of a hundred eighty miles round trip to northern Florida, returning each night to take care of his livestock and crops. "Yes, in the United States, unlike Cuba, farmers can lose their land," he told conference participants. "Drawing from the Cuban people and this revolution has impacted me greatly."

Jacob Perasso. Jacob is a freight rail conductor and member of the SMART-TD union in one of the largest rail yards in the Northeast. He is a leader of the work of the Young Socialists in the US and internationally. He previously worked, among other jobs, in meat-packing plants in the Midwest, where he was involved in a number of union-organizing fights.

Perasso detailed the increasingly dangerous conditions in the rail industry, as bosses reduce crew sizes, extend workdays up to twelve hours, scrimp on training, and demand that workers cut corners on safety. He pointed to the 2013 train derailment in the small town of Lac Mégantic, Quebec, just north of the US-Canada border, where a train loaded with highly flammable petroleum cargo exploded, killing forty-seven people. Especially significant was the refusal of a jury of local residents to convict the two workers the rail company tried to blame for the accident. As evidence of bosses' disregard for safety came out, townspeople had no doubt who was responsible.

Perasso described the system of bonuses, wage differentials, and other incentives the employers use to divide the workforce and get some workers to even help promote increasingly dangerous conditions on the job. Despite such pressures, freight rail workers voted down a contract in 2014 that would have allowed the bosses to begin running one-person train crews. That slowed but didn't stop the owners' offensive.

He pointed to the necessity to transform the unions in the course of struggles through which workers come to increasingly realize their own collective strength. "On the job we seek to explain the history that has brought the labor movement to where it is today," Perasso said. "We explain the need to stop looking to the capitalist owners, their parties, their government, and their state. We need to chart a political course—a course of struggle—independent of them, defending the interests of the entire working class."

Harry D'Agostino. Harry is a worker, bass player, band leader, and Young Socialist. He and his band perform throughout the Northeast and North Central regions of the US. Although he was unable to join the Havana panel at the last minute, his prepared remarks were distributed to those present.

D'Agostino explained that like many millions of young workers he has held numerous jobs, from small shops to warehouses. Also like millions, he's almost always been a "temp worker" who gets no guaranteed hours or days of work, no health coverage, vacation time, or unemployment compensation—and can be fired at any time. Many young workers also struggle under the weight of tens of thousand of dollars of student debt "urged upon us by the government and banks as a way to 'get ahead.'" Most have no hope of ever paying it off, he said.

He described the eye-opening impact of the West Virginia teachers strike, where he and others of his generation saw for the first time the power of the working class in action. "A large-scale workers movement, a social movement across an entire state was entirely new to us," D'Agostino said. "Even more so, a victory was something new. It made it possible to think about fighting and organizing ourselves to emulate that example."

Omari Musa. Omari has worked for half a century in every kind of job, union and nonunion, from rail and oil to an ice cream factory, from California to Miami. He currently lives in Washington, DC, where he is employed by Walmart. He is a lifetime veteran of battles in defense of the rights of African Americans and a longtime national leader of the work to defend the Cuban Revolution, both inside and outside the labor movement.

Musa took up the assertions made by many liberals and radicals in the US that racism is on the rise and that most workers who are Caucasian—the majority of striking teachers in West Virginia and Oklahoma, for example—are reactionary. That's why Donald Trump, not Hillary Clinton, was elected president, they say.

Musa grew up in the deep South under Jim Crow conditions of institutional racial discrimination. He knows the difference between then and now, he said. He pointed to the "social revolution that has taken place in the US," the product of the mass, Black-led movement in the 1950s, '60s, and early '70s that destroyed those institutions of race segregation and profoundly changed the consciousness of working people, both Blacks and Caucasians.

"Today the workforce is more integrated than ever before, and it is harder than at any previous time in US history for the rulers to use racism to divide us," he said. "That social revolution strengthened us all."

Plenty of racial discrimination still exists, he underlined. Such divisions are a source of hundreds of billions in profit and will never be eliminated under capitalism. But racism and anti-Black violence are declining, not growing. "Provocations organized by white-supremacist groups, like the one in Charlottesville, Virginia, in August 2017 draw a few hundred, not thousands as they did only decades ago. Vicious mobs are no longer attacking Blacks in the streets and their homes." One week after the Charlottesville provocation during which one counterdemonstrator was killed, 40,000 people poured into the streets of Boston to repudiate the ultraright action.

Musa pointed to the example of African American football star Colin Kaepernick, who refused to stand during the playing of the national anthem as a protest against police killings and racist attacks. "He became a hero to millions—of all races."

Róger Calero. Róger came to the US from Nicaragua with his family when he was fifteen. He has worked in meatpacking plants in Minnesota and Iowa, where he was a member of the United Food and Commercial Workers and involved in organizing drives and in union struggles defending the rights of immigrant workers. In 2002 the US government arrested and attempted to deport him, triggering a successful international defense effort that won the support of many unions. He was the presidential candidate of the Socialist Workers Party in 2004 and 2008.

Calero focused his remarks on what is at stake for the labor movement in the defense of immigrant workers. He explained what is behind the anti-immigrant drive that has been ratcheted up by the administration of Donald Trump, and how the working class in the United States has been strengthened by the incorporation of millions of foreign-born workers.

The political struggle to win the labor movement and big majority of working people to defend immigrant workers, he said, "is a life-and-death question for the working class." The scapegoating of immigrants is one of the biggest weapons used by the ruling class and both its parties to divide and weaken the working class.

The source of anti-immigrant prejudice, he noted, is not the working class. It's the bosses who promote and benefit from such prejudice, like they profit from discrimination against Blacks and against women. They bring in immigrant labor to increase competition among workers, break unions, drive down wages, and intensify exploitation of the working class as a whole, as they did in the meatpacking industry in the 1980s.

"In the absence of an effective fight by the trade unions to defend the interests of the entire working class—and that includes the effort to organize workers without papers into the unions—this scapegoating of immigrants finds an echo among sections of the working class," Calero noted. "But these attitudes are driven by the competition to sell their labor power, not racism."

The US rulers' objective is not to stop the flow of immigrants, only to regulate it based on their needs, as they have always done. "The vulgar prejudice spewed by President Trump and others around him," Calero noted, "his agitation to 'build the wall,' the brutal detentions, raids, deportations, workplace immigration audits, and other repressive measures are aimed at heightening insecurity and fear among all working people, not immigrant workers alone."

But it is the rulers themselves who are driven by fear, fear of the class battles that are coming and the unity that can be forged by US and foreign-born workers. We have seen this in the meat-packing plants of the Midwest, the coal mines in Utah, and other labor and social struggles.

"The political fight to win amnesty for workers without papers and defend the rights of immigrants is inseparable from the struggle to unify the working class as a whole," Calero said. "It is vital to building a trade union movement that fights for the interests of the entire class."

The fighting history of the United Mine Workers

Radio Havana Cuba

This report on labor struggles waged by the United Mine Workers union in the United States is excerpted from a Radio Havana program that was broadcast worldwide March 27, 1981. The report, in English, aired on the opening day of a strike by 160,000 UMWA miners—a confrontation that over the next ten weeks turned back the bosses' effort to cripple the union.

Calling for solidarity with the miners, the Cuban program highlighted two previous UMWA strikes.

The first, in 1969 in West Virginia, forced the coal bosses to agree to measures that began to curb the devastation of black-lung disease and gave union safety committees more control over work conditions in the mines.

The second, in 1977–78, was the longest coal strike in US history. Miners across the country's coal fields waged a one hundred eleven–day battle, fighting—as Radio Havana notes—to "defend the very existence of their union." In the process, the miners defied Democratic president James

Carter's order to return to work under the Taft-Hartley "Slave Labor" Act.

In 1935 the United Mine Workers was the largest and most powerful industrial union in the United States. Coal miners were the only workers who successfully organized racially integrated locals in the South before 1900 and became the first industrial workers to establish the eight-hour day in 1898.

After it had been almost destroyed in the 1920s, the UMW reorganized itself between 1933 and 1935 and became the backbone for the founding of the Congress of Industrial Organizations (CIO). Coal miners provided both money and organizers for a drive to unionize the nation's basic industries.

Miners were among the few workers who fought their employers openly during World War II.

There were two major UMW strikes in recent history of tremendous political importance. In 1969 and 1978 coal miners took on every issue of concern to US workers: health, safety, benefits, wages, inflation, and especially the viability of the rank-and-file movement in the survival of a strong trade union.

In February and March 1969, West Virginia miners led the way when 95 percent of the state's twenty-five thousand miners stayed out of the pits for more than three weeks. They forced the state legislature to pass a new coal mine health and safety law.

Later that year President Richard Nixon considered vetoing the National Coal Mine Health and Safety Act. But miners threatened another strike and forced him to sign the historic law, which, for the first time, provided compensation to victims of black lung disease.

The Black Lung Association, which rank-and-file miners

"West Virginia, the historic heart of coal country in the United States, has been the site of some of the hardest fought labor battles in US history."

Top: March 1981. Coal miners protest in Washington a few weeks before 160,000 miners launched strike that pushed back employers' concession demands. Black lung, the deadly disease driven back by actions of miners and their communities in 1960s, '70s, and '80s, is again on rise today as bosses boost coal production and profits with new technology and mine community health clinics, previously funded by the mine companies, have closed.

Bottom: United Mine Workers members and supporters shut down Pittston coal plant in Virginia during 11-month strike in 1989.

"Coal miners organized racially integrated locals in the South before 1900 and became the first industrial workers to establish the eight-hour day in 1898," the Radio Havana broadcast explained. "In strikes in the 1960s and 1970s, miners took on every issue of concern to US workers: health, safety, benefits, wages, inflation, and the survival of a strong union."

"Coal miners were among the few workers who fought their employers openly during World War II," Radio Havana reported.

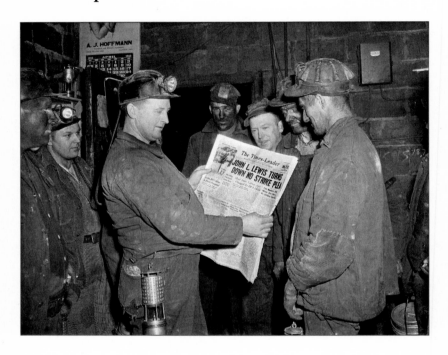

In 1943 miners waged four national strikes to oppose the imperialist government's wartime wage freeze and bosses' dangerous speedup and disregard for safety. They rejected no-strike pledge the US government had won from union officials in virtually every other industry.

Above: Miners in Ohio, 1943, read headline reporting UMWA president John L. Lewis' defiance of government threat to use troops to replace striking miners during World War II. "You can't mine coal with bayonets!" miners replied.

formed in January 1969 to sponsor and push for the West Virginia law, soon became an advocate for the interests of working and retired miners within a union whose leaders had sold out to the companies.

The strike also inspired Joseph "Jock" Yablonski to challenge Tony Boyle for the union's presidency. Running on the slogan "Boyle's in bed with the coal operators," Yablonski ran a strong campaign and vowed to continue the fight beyond the December elections. He was assassinated by Boyle-hired gunmen on the last of the year but at his funeral Miners for Democracy (MFD) was formed.

In June 1970, a third rank-and-file organization was born out of another strike in southern West Virginia, the Disabled Miners and Widows of Southern West Virginia. These three groups united to back the Miners for Democracy slate at a West Virginia convention in May 1972.

In December UMW members elected nine rank-and-file miners [from the MFD slate] to the international office for the first time in the union's history.

The union was tremendously strengthened by the electoral victory. Now all officers in the union's twenty-one districts must answer to the rank and file at union election time. Under Boyle, only four districts had full autonomy.

The 1972 MFD slate stood on a platform which called for election of district officials and executive board members, rank-and-file ratification of contracts, no firings for refusal to work in unsafe conditions, a full-time safety committeeman in each mine, national and district support of local disputes, no discrimination in hiring and firing, uniform enforcement of the contract, increased pensions for retired miners, and responsible management of the welfare funds. It also pledged to reduce the salaries of top union officials.

Boyle was ousted by MFD candidate Arnold Miller, a victim of black lung and a former miner—an electrician with twenty-four years on the job. A new regime set in.

In 1974, miners voted to ratify their contract for the first time in the union's eighty-four-year history. A small group of handpicked negotiators could no longer sell out the interests of thousands of miners in smoke-filled rooms, hundreds of miles from the coal fields.

Coal miners continued to demonstrate their militancy during the summers of 1975, '76, and '77. Local disputes which began in southern West Virginia in 1975 and 1976 flared up into coal-field-wide strikes both years, because miners were so dissatisfied with the way the operators were refusing to deal with grievances at the mines. Instead of discussing disputes, the companies tried to force miners back to work with federal injunctions, fines, arrests, and threatened firings.

In 1975, eighty thousand miners struck. In 1976, a hundred twenty thousand did—nearly every union miner east of the Mississippi. The 1976 strike was so effective that federal judges in Charleston, West Virginia, withdrew their fines and injunctions, an event almost unique in modern labor history.

Then in 1977, miners struck again in protest over cutbacks in their medical benefits, so important in a dangerous industry centered in southern Appalachia, where hospitals refuse to admit patients without cash on the spot to pay for emergency care.

Then in 1978 the UMW strike emerged as the central class question in the United States. The coal miners were fighting for the very existence of their union and every other union in the nation.

The attack on the UMW was part of the offensive being waged against the entire labor movement. That year saw the formation of the Council for a Union-Free Environment of the National Association of Manufacturers. The year before, the steel companies organized a drive to defeat the rank-and-file candidate for the presidency of the United Steel Workers [Ed Sadlowski].

The main reason the corporations were determined to take on the miners was to discredit and crush the rank-and-file struggle for democracy in the union. The collective bargaining which went on before and during the strike reflected a new trend.

Industry is now coming to the bargaining table armed with its own set of demands to take away already existing gains and determined not to make concessions. It's a give-back policy that's cropping up in other industry negotiations.

Under capitalism workers are forced to fight for everything they get. It's either fight or go backward.

Though the miners did not totally succeed in stopping this trend they were victorious in certain key areas. The corporations failed in their central aim, which was to actually destroy the UMW. The miners also successfully defended their right to strike, and seriously weakened the strikebreaking Taft-Hartley Act. Moreover, their effort had far-reaching positive effects on the rest of the labor movement.

When the UMW negotiation team sat down at the bargaining table in Washington, they were ostensibly dealing with coal operators. In the past, that term referred to coal-mining companies, but the industry's chief negotiator was Joseph P. Brennan, who really represents the gigantic multinationals controlled by superbankers.

The biggest coal company, Peabody, is controlled completely by the Kennecott Copper Company, which in turn is dominated by the Morgan bankers and Guggenheims.

The next biggest coal company, Consolidation, is owned by the Continental Oil Company, a multibillion-dollar asset with holdings in Africa and other overseas lands. Continental was part of Rockefeller's Standard Oil Company before the trust's nominal dissolution in 1911. Its control is now divided between the Rockefellers and Morgan bankers, with the Pittsburgh Mellons having a secondary voice.

The third biggest company, Island Creek, is owned by the Occidental Oil Company. Then there are the big mining properties of the US Steel Corporation, which was founded by J.P. Morgan, Bethlehem Steel, and many coal companies owned entirely by Exxon, Mobil Oil, Gulf Oil, other oil giants, and the big utilities.

It was the amassed power of the monopolists that confronted the miners as they began their strike.

The miners' struggle of 1978 created a new situation in the trade union movement. It gave a real jolt to big business's drive for take-away contracts. It blunted the vicious antilabor campaign launched against all labor organizations. By ignoring government attempts to break the strike with the Taft-Hartley injunction, it landed a warning blow at that dangerous piece of antilabor legislation.

Defense of labor's basic right to strike had positive repercussions among workers in all industries. In the process of the strike, the need for public ownership of the mines and coal resources became a hot issue in the minds of many workers. Why should such vital natural resources be under the control of the big oil, utility, and steel companies, and the big bankers?

In 1978, the United Mine Workers of America's strike brought out once again the well-known fact that under capitalism workers are forced to fight for everything they get. It's either fight or go backward. The miners have proven it takes a fight to win.

INDEX

Tribunes of the People and the Trade Unions

V.I. Lenin, Leon Trotsky, Farrell Dobbs, Jack Barnes, Karl Marx

"Our ideal should not be the trade union secretary, but *the tribune of the people,* able to react to every manifestation of tyranny and oppression."
V.I. Lenin, 1902

"Leon Trotsky was concerned with the revolutionary mobilization of the working class; he followed with interest strategy and tactics in the trade unions."
Farrell Dobbs, 1969

"With revolutionary leadership, the unions can lead workers and their allies in city, town, and country—farmers; small producers; tradespeople, drivers and other owner-operators— to political independence from the ruling class."
Jack Barnes, 2018

Building trade unions is an irreplaceable part of unifying the working class and forging a proletarian party. With the class-collaborationist course of the current officialdom, unions can't organize working people effectively to fight the capitalists' assault on living conditions and job safety, much less their government and its murderous wars.

Workers and their allies need a line of march to win state power from the exploiters and establish a workers and farmers government. To do that a revolutionary workers party is needed—a party of tribunes of the people.

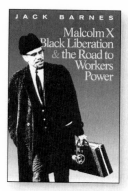

FOR FURTHER READING

The Clintons' anti-working-class record

WHY WASHINGTON FEARS WORKING PEOPLE

JACK BARNES

The Clintons' Anti-Working-Class Record

Why Washington Fears Working People

JACK BARNES

Describes the profit-driven course of Democrats and Republicans alike, and the political awakening of workers seeking to understand and resist these assaults. $10. Also in Spanish, French, and Farsi.

Are They Rich Because They're Smart?

Class, Privilege, and Learning under Capitalism

JACK BARNES

Exposes the self-serving rationalizations by well-paid middle-class layers that their intelligence and schooling equip them to "regulate" workers' lives. Includes "Capitalism, the Working Class, and the Transformation of Learning." $10. Also in Spanish, French, and Farsi.

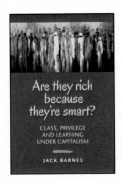

Are they rich because they're smart?

CLASS, PRIVILEGE AND LEARNING UNDER CAPITALISM

JACK BARNES

Is Socialist Revolution in the US Possible?

A Necessary Debate among Working People

MARY-ALICE WATERS

An unhesitating "Yes"—that's the answer given here. Possible—but not inevitable. That depends on what working people *do*. $10. Also in Spanish, French, and Farsi.

Is socialist revolution in the US possible?

A NECESSARY DEBATE AMONG WORKING PEOPLE

MARY-ALICE WATERS

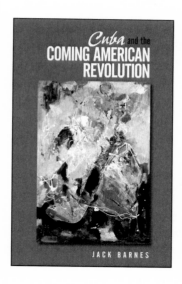

Cuba and the Coming American Revolution

JACK BARNES

This is a book about the struggles of working people in the imperialist heartland, the youth attracted to them, and the example set by the Cuban people that revolution is not only necessary—it can be made. It is about the class struggle in the US, where the revolutionary capacities of workers and farmers are today as utterly discounted by the ruling powers as were those of the Cuban toilers. And just as wrongly. $10. Also in Spanish, French, and Farsi.

"It's the Poor Who Face the Savagery of the US 'Justice' System"

The Cuban Five Talk about Their Lives within the US Working Class

How US cops, courts, and prisons work as "an enormous machine for grinding people up." Five Cuban revolutionaries framed up and held in US jails for 16 years explain the human devastation of capitalist "justice"—and how socialist Cuba is different. $15. Also in Spanish, Farsi, and Greek.

Puerto Rico: Independence Is a Necessity

RAFAEL CANCEL MIRANDA

One of the five Puerto Rican Nationalists imprisoned by Washington for more than 25 years and released in 1979 speaks out on the brutal reality of US colonial domination, the example of Cuba's socialist revolution, and the ongoing struggle for independence. $6. Also in Spanish and Farsi.

ALSO FROM PATHFINDER

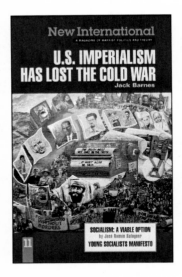

U.S. Imperialism Has Lost the Cold War

JACK BARNES

The collapse of regimes across Eastern Europe and the USSR claiming to be communist did not mean workers and farmers there had been defeated. In today's sharpening capitalist conflicts and wars, these toilers have joined working people the world over in the class struggle against exploitation. In *New International* no. 11. $16. Also in Spanish, French, Farsi, and Greek.

Cuba and Angola: The War for Freedom

HARRY VILLEGAS ("POMBO")

The story of Cuba's unparalleled contribution to the fight to free Africa from the scourge of apartheid. And how, in the doing, Cuba's socialist revolution was strengthened. $10. Also in Spanish.

Cosmetics, Fashions, and the Exploitation of Women

JOSEPH HANSEN, EVELYN REED, MARY-ALICE WATERS

How big business plays on women's second-class status and economic insecurities to market cosmetics and rake in profits. And how the entry of millions of women into the workforce has irreversibly changed relations between women and men—for the better. $15. Also in Spanish and Farsi.

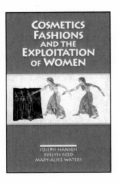

Malcolm X Talks to Young People

"The young generation of whites, Blacks, browns, whatever else there is—you're living at a time of revolution," Malcolm said in December 1964. "And I for one will join in with anyone, I don't care what color you are, as long as you want to change this miserable condition that exists on this earth." $15. Also in Spanish, French, Farsi, and Greek.

Thomas Sankara Speaks

The Burkina Faso Revolution, 1983–87

Under Sankara's guidance, Burkina Faso's revolutionary government led peasants, workers, women, and youth to expand literacy; to sink wells, plant trees, erect housing; to combat women's oppression; to carry out land reform; to join others in Africa and worldwide to free themselves from the imperialist yoke. $24. Also in French.

Art and Revolution

Writings on Literature, Politics, and Culture

LEON TROTSKY

One of the outstanding revolutionary leaders of the 20th century examines the place and aesthetic independence of art, literature, and artistic expression in the struggle for a new, socialist society. $22

REVOLUTIONARY LEADERS IN THEIR OWN WORDS

The Communist Manifesto

KARL MARX AND
FREDERICK ENGELS

Why communism is not a set of preconceived principles but the line of march of the working class toward power, "springing from an existing class struggle, a historical movement going on under our very eyes." The founding document of the modern revolutionary workers movement. $5. Also in Spanish, French, Farsi, and Arabic.

Lenin's Final Fight

Speeches and Writings, 1922–23

V.I. LENIN

In 1922 and 1923, V.I. Lenin, central leader of the world's first socialist revolution, waged what was to be his last political battle—one that was lost following his death. At stake was whether that revolution, and the international communist movement it led, would remain on the proletarian course that had brought workers and peasants to power in October 1917. $20. Also in Spanish and Greek.

The History of the Russian Revolution

LEON TROTSKY

How, under Lenin's leadership, the Bolshevik Party led millions of workers and farmers to overthrow the state power of the landlords and capitalists in 1917 and bring to power a government that advanced their class interests at home and worldwide. Unabridged, 3 vols. in one. Written by one of the central leaders of that socialist revolution. $38. Also in French and Russian.

Socialism on Trial
Testimony at Minneapolis Sedition Trial
JAMES P. CANNON
The revolutionary program of the working class, as presented in response to frame-up charges of "seditious conspiracy" in 1941, on the eve of US entry into World War II. The defendants were leaders of the Minneapolis labor movement and the Socialist Workers Party. $16. Also in Spanish, French, and Farsi.

In Defense of Socialism
Four Speeches on the 30th Anniversary of the Cuban Revolution, 1988–89
FIDEL CASTRO

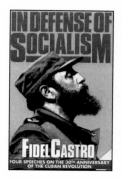

Castro describes the decisive place of volunteer Cuban fighters in the final stage of the war in Angola against invading forces of South Africa's apartheid regime. Not only is economic and social progress possible without capitalism's dog-eat-dog competition, the Cuban leader says, but socialism is humanity's only way forward. $15

Our Politics Start with the World
JACK BARNES

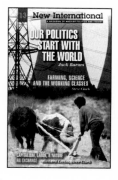

The huge economic and cultural inequalities between imperialist and semicolonial countries, and among classes within them, are accentuated by the workings of capitalism. To build parties able to lead a successful revolutionary struggle for power in our own countries, vanguard workers must be guided by a strategy to close this gap. In *New International* no. 13. $14. Also in Spanish, French, Farsi, and Greek.